I Hate My Job

*How to Quit Your Job by
Creating an Exit Strategy,
Sticking to a Timeline,
and Handing in
Your Resignation*

by Geoffrey Wright

Table of Contents

Introduction

This book will provide you with a step-by-step guide to quit the job that you dislike, and create a solid plan to get the career that you want instead. This book will help you develop the perfect exit strategy, which even includes the final to-do list you'll leave for your boss, and how to make sure that you land in (or create) your dream job after your resignation.

This book is written for anyone currently facing a career crisis and looking to make some major changes in their life. If you are one of the millions of people who know that your current job just isn't fulfilling, then this book will help you learn to follow your heart to get one step closer to achieving your ultimate happiness. At the same time, you will also find numerous tips within each chapter that will help you identify the characteristics of a job you'd actually never want to quit. This book will help you to finally take control over your own career choices by knowing what your new job should give you that your current job simply can't.

Before you continue reading, reflect for just a moment on the basic fact that you are not currently fulfilled in your job, and therefore you're considering (and looking forward to) a major life change. If you are ready to finally take the reins away from your employer, and start deciding for yourself on what truly works for you, then this book is for you!

Chapter 1: Know When You've Had Enough

Everybody has had an experience of a dreary Monday, or "a case of the Mondays." You might have felt that Monday is the most terrible day of the week, because you have to face the commute, your dreadful cubicle, and your annoying coworker or boss first thing in the morning. And there's a whole week of the same still ahead of you. The idea of having to wake up in the morning and face these things again can make you feel uninspired, frustrated, and sometimes even downright sick.

It's Probably Not You.

It sometimes can be hard to identify the source of these negative feelings, and some people even start to believe that maybe they're just lazy and wouldn't want to work anywhere. They tell themselves that it's not the job they hate so much, it's just 'work' in general. Or, like the millions of people out there that just go into their office daily as if they are zombies, you might not fully understand the exact reasons why you do not love what you do anymore. But the bottom line is this: The problem isn't you. It's that you simply don't like your job (whatever the reason may be).

There are a lot of good reasons why employees might leave their job. If you have a feeling that your job just isn't right for you anymore, check to see if your reasons might be included on this list. If they are, then you need to buckle in and prepare yourself for a career shift.

1. Your company is sinking.

You might have become unmotivated if you feel that your employer does not know where the company is going anymore. That is likely to happen if your company has recently lost its credibility, or if it is beginning to sink deeper in debt. It is quite natural for employees to feel compelled to leave their jobs if their employer cannot guarantee them job security or career growth anymore.

2. You have an irreparable relationship with your manager or boss.

If you are having a hard time dealing with your supervisor, and you think that his actions at the workplace are making your life more difficult, you have a good reason to resign, especially if you have tried doing your part in repairing your relationship. If you cannot trust that your manager you're your back and looks out for your best interest, then unless you can predict that he or she might soon leave, it's better to be proactive and move to another department or workplace.

You may also feel that you are being undervalued by your direct supervisor and there is no positive way to get his or her attention. You feel that you are not likely to be chosen for the next promotion even if you are doing your best. If you think that your boss does not consider you to be a key member of the team, then you may choose to go somewhere else where you can feel valued.

3. Your work does not support your life needs.

If your work does not allow you to have time with your family or attend to personal leisure from time to time, you may find that you need a job that works within the confines of your personal goals and lifestyle. This holds true especially if you are very aware that you are working for the sole purpose of making your home life more comfortable. If you can't even enjoy your home life because of work, then what's the point of having that job?

4. Your values go against the company's culture.

If your belief systems are definitely at odds with your company's value set, then it may feel as if you have to drag your feet through the front office door each day. You will find that it is difficult to work diligently when you question the major goals that your company strives to achieve, and you will soon wake up and know that your company will never change to adapt to your set of beliefs.

5. You do not think that your company employs consistent policies.

Consistency is the key to employee retention. If you think that your company is willing to make exceptions to its policies to cater to certain employees or certain situations, you may tend to question your company's ethics. That story is the same if you think that your company lists honesty as its core value but concurrently hides something important from the clients. When you are beginning to question your company's integrity because of its inability to stick to its own rules, you may feel inclined to quit your job, and rightfully so.

6. You don't get along with your colleagues.

If there are times when you feel like you don't even care if you burn bridges with your coworkers because you simply do not like them, then you might not even feel like going to work at all. One of the major reasons why happy employees appreciate their job is because they appreciate their peers, and if you think that you do not have friends at work or you feel like an outcast, it becomes easy to think that nobody understands or appreciates you. If you've done your part to be kind to them, yet it just isn't working, you may choose to leave your job and look for a sense of belongingness somewhere else.

7. You have stopped enjoying it.

You may not even have enjoyed your job at all since your first day. It could be that you find your job to be monotonous, and that you're stuck in a rut. It may be that your job doesn't challenge you in any way, and when you think about your job, you feel the dread of having to experience incredible boredom for a prolonged period of time. Or, you may have realized that your skills and your interests simply match another job that you would prefer to have instead.

The bottom line is this: the moment you started looking for reasons to quit your job, then you have already subconsciously decided that you do not want to wake up and continue going to that office anymore. That is the telltale sign that your job simply does not work for you anymore.

In this situation, there are exactly three options you must choose among:

1. You can stay and remain unhappy, (in which case, I assure you that you'll be reading this book again in a year or two); or

2. You can stay and force yourself to address or adapt to the challenges that you face in the workplace; or

3. You can quit your job and find something else to do.

For the sake of your own sanity, it is a much better idea that you resign from work, and find something else to do with the potential of making you feel happier and more fulfilled. This will relieve you of a great deal of stress and make you stop worrying about being unproductive, restless, and downright miserable at work. At the same time, you will be able to broaden your choices and find a suitable job that would give you personal fulfillment. Also, this process of change may bring about some substantial personal growth in way you might not have predicted.

Chapter 2: Adapting the Right Mindset

When you're thinking that you don't want to go to work anymore, there are probably different thoughts going through your mind. You might begin to worry that you could be leaving the best opportunity that you've had so far, and that you just need to shake off your negativity, get yourself together, and rekindle your relationship with your company.

However, what you are experiencing is probably just your fear of the unknown, because you don't know what you are going to do next. You are probably worrying about your boss' reaction, or that you might be leaving the only friends that you have, or the only type of work you feel qualified to do. You might even be reluctant because the thought of writing your resignation letter seems difficult simply because you don't know exactly how to explain yourself.

But there is no point in worrying about all the little negative details, and all the bad things that may or may not happen. What you need now is a healthy mindset to help you realign your life goals and plan the next steps that you need to take in order to get your career and life back on track. While you are still thinking about quitting your job but haven't done anything about it yet, this is a good time to identify your goals.

Knowing What You Need Out of Life

At this point, you may be trying to figure out what has changed in your life that made you decide to change how you make a living. Quitting a job is a big decision, and you need to think it through – losing a job is a risk, no matter how you look at it. On the other hand, it is also the perfect opportunity to reflect on your personal goals, and take a much-needed step forward in your life. Surely by now you've realized your job is not meeting some of the most important goals that you have set for yourself, which is why you tend to think that you are better off without it. Before you resign from your workplace though, think carefully about the things that you want to get.

Here is one way to help clearly define your goals:

Picture an older version of yourself, facing retirement for example. What are the things you believe you should have accomplished by then? Do you see yourself living the jetsetter and adventuresome lifestyle on your own? Or do you foresee a future with children that have finished college and earning a living professionally? Do you think that by that age you should have published a book or sold a painting? Or do you think that by that age you should have created a multi-million dollar corporation that your children may soon inherit? These goals and visions of your future will largely affect the career and life choices you need to make well in advance (now).

Next, start to think about the immediate future. To make it easier, here is a list of questions you should answer to help plan your goals and action steps for the next few months and years.

1. What is your current living situation, and how might you be able to improve it in the near future? Do you wish to acquire property? Do you own your own home? Do you have mortgages or car loans?

2. Do you have a family that you need to support that requires you to have a stable source of income?

3. Do you have any special skills, portfolio or work, or a list of accomplishments that would assist you in selling yourself and your capabilities easily?

4. Do you have any particular passion that you wish to pursue? What would you do with your time if money wasn't a factor?

5. Do you have a backup job in mind, or temporary part time work that could help you pay your bills during a transition period?

6. How much money do you have saved up to sustain yourself while you are in between jobs (or while you are starting your own company)?

The answers to these questions will help you think about the direction and appropriate course of action to ensure that you still maintain your personal comforts and address your commitments while you are still deciding what to do next. The answers will also help you gauge your ability to move into your next career choice with peace of mind.

The Best Case Scenario

Ideally, you'll want to quit your current job only after you've already lined up a new job (or started your own company on the side and drummed up enough work to sustain yourself on your own). In this scenario, you would give your current employer notice, celebrate your last day there a couple weeks later, and then start work immediately at your new place of employment. This way, there's no gap in your income, and you'll smoothly and successfully have transitioned into a more tolerable work environment. This "ideal" or "best case" scenario implies that you will have spent quite a large amount of time outside your normal working hours preparing for your next position, submitting job applications to other companies, preparing for interviews, and then sneaking in interviews whenever you can. Another benefit of this situation is that because you still have a job, you will be in a better position to negotiate a higher salary during your interviews because you will appear less "desperate." Your interviewers will know that you're not in dire need for a new job because you are currently working, therefore strategically you can use this to your advantage to secure a better pay rate.

However, this "best case" scenario isn't always the reality. Sometimes the feeling of being drained from your current employment situation prevents you from being able to put your best foot forward. Or the time spent at work prevents you from being available enough to appropriately figure out what you want to do next and take the appropriate steps to get there.

Mentally Preparing Yourself for the Future

Once you've decided that you need to quit your job no matter what, even if you haven't yet lined up your next move, here are things to do to ensure you have the right mindset to prepare for resignation.

1. Check your available funds and make sure that you are financially equipped to temporarily go through unemployment, or a period of transitional uncertainty. Keep in mind that it may take you three to six months before you get another job, so make sure that you can support yourself for this period of time with your savings alone. Knowing that you have this kind of support will allow you to focus on your goals instead of just jumping from one job to another to sustain yourself.

Note: If you want to quit your job but you don't think you've saved enough to prepare yourself for temporary unemployment, consider augmenting your income first before quitting your regular work. Take an extra job, if possible a freelance gig that is enjoyable enough to make working after hours not so intolerable. This would allow you not only to take your mind off the stress from your primary workplace, but it will also ensure that you can have the necessary period of financial stability once you have finally resigned from work. If you decide to do this, run some calculations and set a monetary goal and a timeframe during which you can achieve this, to ensure this situation is only temporary. By being able to countdown and see the light at the end of the tunnel, this double-work scenario will be much more tolerable.

2. Review your immediate needs and financial obligations. If you can still attend to them without your job, your decision to quit your job will be much easier. Make a list of your regular bills and financial obligations. If you don't think you can afford to give up your job, then don't quit quite yet. Instead, as mentioned above, consider working temporarily after hours to augment your income in order to pick up the pace of payments until you can afford a period of time with less or no income.

3. Identify your strengths, and list all the possible jobs that you might be good at, with or without experience. List all the jobs that might help you feel fulfilled in some way that you're currently not now. Imagine the perfect workplace for you – think of the best compensation and management scenario that could be matched to your skill sets and experience. That way, you will always have a vision of the best workplace scenario and best compensation package possible. When you have that in mind, you will never sell yourself short again.

4. If you are supporting a family, and you know that they might worry about your decision, consult with them and tell them about your plans and reasons why you are quitting. Since you are under an obligation to support them, assure them that you will still be able to provide for their needs, or instead consider asking them for commitment to support your decision by

encouraging them to find extra income for the household for at least a temporary period of time. Although you may not want to rely this for any significant period of time, especially if you've always been the breadwinner, it doesn't hurt to ask for others to pitch in temporarily while you make a transition that will ultimately be better for the whole family.

5. Remember why you're doing this. Keep in mind that your sense of personal integrity is being affected negatively by having to continually go to work at a job that you simply aren't passionate about. Remember that personal growth often comes in the face of challenge and tough decisions. Think of how important happiness and fulfillment is to you. Feel confident in the realization that this is something that simply must change. There is no other option, and no looking back. Move forward with the faith and confidence that this is what's ultimately best for you and your family.

Once you are better mentally prepared to take the step of resigning from your job in search of a better life, the next chapter will discuss how to make your resignation go as smoothly as possible.

Chapter 3: Creating a Timeline, and Sticking to It

Once you've committed to the decision that your current job just isn't right for you, and it never will be, you have then realized that you need to leave, and there is no other option. That can be easier said than done sometimes, though.

Although you may be waiting to finish a certain project or task before you leave, or you may be waiting until you get your next paycheck, or you may just be waiting until the boss seems to be in a good mood before you notify him or her. There will always be a reason or excuse to stay just a little bit longer. For this reason, the best thing you can do is to actually create a timeline, in writing, for yourself. Then you must stick to it without wavering.

It's important to realize there never will be that perfect time to go, and that each day you're still there is one less day that you could be somewhere else, doing something that you enjoy a whole lot more. Life is short – why waste any time?

So, get out that piece of paper right now (yes, I'm talking to you). And let's write down some dates.

First, write down the date that you made this decision. This date should represent the very day you knew for a fact that your job does not give you what you need to be fulfilled and happy, and therefore you need to find something else to do instead. Next to that date, write down something to the effect of "The Date I Decided and Committed to Quitting."

Next, pinpoint an actual calendar date that, in your mind, feels "soon enough" to be your last day, but not one that makes you absolutely panic because it seems "too soon." Again, we're looking for a date in the range between "too soon" and "soon enough." This may seem abstract, but go with your gut feeling. Don't think too much about any specific tasks you have going on at work, but just focus on your own emotional wellbeing for now. This date that you choose will be "the light at the end of the tunnel," so to speak. And every day between now and then won't seem too bad anymore, because you know the end is near so all the little things at work that used to get under your skin can now make you smile to yourself, knowing that you won't have to tolerate it much longer. Once you've selected a date, write next to it "My Last Day at Work." Congratulations, you just identified your last day at your job! Doesn't that feel good?

Finally, count backwards from that date, by the amount of time your company requires you to give advanced notice, which is typically two weeks. (You can find this information in your employee handbook). If you are feeling generous, then add an extra week, so your employer actually has three weeks' notice instead of two to find your replacement. Next to this date, write "I Will Hand in My Resignation."

Now, at the bottom of this sheet of paper, write the following:

"I, [insert your name here], acknowledge that I am not happy or fulfilled at my job, and I deserve the chance to find a different way to earn a living that will also make me feel happy and fulfilled. In order to do that, I must quit my job. Although this may be difficult, I am making a commitment to myself, my happiness, and my future. I promise to myself that I will stick to these dates, and will not waiver from this decision."

Last, sign the piece of paper and date it. You've now made a contract with yourself, and for the sake of your own wellbeing, you should stick to it. Post this contract somewhere visible in your home, or keep it in your purse or wallet. Or better yet, add these dates to your schedule or calendar, if you keep one.

Chapter 4: How to Quit Your Job

Even if you hate going to work, you still want to make sure that your former employer does not hate you back, especially if you are gunning for a place in a similar line of work. The world is small, and you should avoid burning a bridge that you don't have to. Be mature, professional, and courteous in all aspects of leaving your current company, and keep their best interest in mind too. Therefore, the right thing to do is to let them know right away once you've decided to quit. This doesn't mean you will have to leave exactly two weeks later. Many companies will allow you to stay longer if that's what you prefer, as long as you work with them to schedule the date of your departure. Also, if you want a slower "transition" out, many companies would consider allowing you to cut down to part-time work, which will give you more time to figure out and work towards your next move in life, while still providing a source of income to support yourself during this period.

In any case, by being respectful of your employer, they will be more likely to be respectful and helpful toward you. Be sure to do your part in facilitating positive interactions throughout your departure process.

Here are some things you should do in order to make sure that you can get a good letter of recommendation from your boss, any outstanding back pay, and that if the worst-case scenario were to occur, your old company would still welcome you back.

1. Tell your boss that you are quitting in advance.

Most companies require two weeks' notice or more before an employee can resign. That gives your office enough time to find someone that can take your place. At the same time, that allows you to finish any task that you may be working on, or at least get to a good stopping point.

It is very important when giving this notice to give your company that you express your gratitude for your time there, and that you value them as a company even though you have decided to leave. Be prepared for the scenario that when your supervisor then realizes that some of your needs are not being fulfilled, he or she may attempt to remedy the situation by offering incentives to stay and/or the opportunity to voice your concerns. Be prepared to explain the general reasons why you've decided to leave, but only do so if explicitly asked. It's best to practice in advance how you might express your grievances in a polite and respectful way.

2. Turn over everything, and be as helpful as possible.

If you still have tasks that need to be completed, make sure that you accomplish them, or at least prepare instructions for your replacement to be able to easily take over these tasks. Also, voluntarily return everything the company has lent you – that way, you will be perceived as an honest person, and you won't be bothered later by the human resource department regarding the company phone or other equipment you still have.

3. Do not badmouth your company.

Employers often doubt applicants that tend to say bad things about their previous place of employment – if you speak poorly about your old job or colleagues, your interviewers might wonder what would prevent you from speaking poorly about your next job? Even if you are having a hard time at work, avoid telling people that you have been mistreated by your employer, unless it calls for a legal case and you need support. That way, you can be sure that you won't burn the bridges behind you, and you won't be facing any possible libel suits.

Taking these precautionary steps will ensure that any potential future employer won't hear negative things about you, and at the same time, will ensure to your old company that you have a sense of responsibility and integrity. This will not only help you get powerful recommendation letters, but also lets your former employer realize that it is their loss that you are quitting, not yours.

The next chapter will help you announce your resignation while still keeping your employer happy.

Chapter 5: The Art of Resigning

Telling your boss that you are quitting is the highlight of the entire resignation process. You may have dreamed about this moment, and have all sorts of visions of how it could play out. This is also the part where you may face objections, questions, and incentives from your employer, which may make the idea of resigning hard for you. However, if you have already made up your mind, be sure that you resign with class.

Why Not Go AWOL Instead?

While there are not many legal repercussions for employees who go AWOL, it's not a good idea because it could damage your reputation as mentioned in the previous chapter. If you leave your employment in bad faith, the employer would have a reason to pursue legal action that may hurt your attempt to work elsewhere. You do not want to receive a phone call asking you to hand over documents that you have mistakenly taken home just when you are ready to move on. That would only make things awkward when you run into your old boss again.

Even if you are about to be fired, it's still better to resign with a letter or in person verbally. This way, you can still take advantage of your employment benefits, such as cashing in on unused vacation leave, back pay, and letters of recommendation.

How to Resign Tactfully

When you consider the very nature of resigning, you may feel that it's difficult to end an employee-employer relationship without either of you harboring ill feelings against each other. For that reason, having a letter of resignation is the best option.

A letter of resignation serves as a legal document that serves as a record explaining that you are terminating your relationship with the company. More importantly, this letter allows you to say things that you may not be able to comfortably or easily say verbally to your previous employer. It allows you to focus on your resignation and state your intentions clearly, without meeting any objections or unwanted reactions.

So, what do you say when you are resigning? Well, keep it very short, say that you have decided to leave and provide a timeframe for your intended departure date. You don't have an obligation to elaborate your reasons why you're leaving. To lessen the blow, make the letter sound as positive as possible by expressing your gratitude and mentioning that you've had many good experiences there, and explain that the company has helped you grow in your career. If you feel that you really do need to express the reason why you are leaving, do so in no more than two sentences. If you have too many reasons, only state the "safe" ones, such as an issue with not having enough personal time, or too long of a commute and wanting to find a job closer to home, etc. If the reason you're leaving involves animosity with the employer or your coworkers, you may want to leave that out.

If there is no way to resign by handing in your resignation letter, use email or the telephone instead. However, you should be aware that these methods are considered informal, and the employer may prefer that you resign in person. These methods are nonetheless handy if you feel that it would be unhealthy for you to face your boss again, or if other circumstances do not allow you to physically resign.

Other Things to Remember

1. Once your employer has received your resignation, you are not required to stay longer than the amount of notice stated in your letter, even if your boss requests it. You can move on anytime after you have

fulfilled the length of time provided in your letter of resignation, as long as it meets the minimum per your original employment agreement or employee handbook.

2. Should you resign because you already have another job and therefore were unable to give proper notice, you can offer to work after hours until the position is filled. Should your employer accept that compromise, be sure that this agreement is documented in writing that you will be paid for the rendered hours.

3. Ask to participate in an exit interview or "debriefing." This will allow you to review your employment contract and be aware of any details regarding when and how you will receive your last salary payment and encashment of any unused leave. At the same time, make sure that you know all the employee benefits that you are still entitled to after your last day at work. If you have a company 401k account, find out how to roll that into your personal accounts, and what paperwork you'll need from your employer.

After these steps, you can now consider yourself fully resigned from your company. The next chapter will help you find another job, preferably a job that is much more aligned with your skills, interests, and lifestyle; and one that may give you a sense of fulfillment and happiness also.

Chapter 6: Getting the Perfect Job

Now that you have identified your goals and you've paved the way to leave your current position, you now have the opportunity to find the job that perfectly fits your profile. Again, in the best case or "ideal" scenario, you will actually find and secure your dream job while still employed at your old place of work, and resign only after you have your new job offer in writing. But in any case, when looking for a new job, here are things you need to make sure that your new workplace is willing to provide for you:

1. Opportunity to grow

Only choose a job that will allow you to climb the career ladder while also learning and developing new skills. Not only will this allow you to provide new meat and potatoes to your resume, but it also ensures that your job is challenging enough for you to prevent burnout.

2. Opportunity to be recognized

If one of the reasons why you left your former job is that you do not feel particularly essential to your company, or properly valued as a skilled employee, then be sure to find a job where you can shine in your workplace. That means that you need to find a position that allows you to perform well and is within your niche.

3. Freedom to express yourself

It is ideal for you to find a job that would allow you to wear your preferred style of clothing, practice (or at least not inhibit) your religion or belief system, or at least allow you to make suggestions to management. A diverse work environment that is accepting of its employees and their opinions can be beneficial to the company. This is an ideal situation, and more and more companies are moving in this direction. By seeking out a position at this type of company, you will never feel that your personality is not welcomed in your job.

4. Harmony between your personal values and the company's goals

It is very important that you have a job that allows you to work without the feeling that you are going against your own set of beliefs or values. It's important that you believe in the integrity of your work and in the importance of your workplace in your personal growth. At the same time, it should make you feel that your work is something that allows and helps you to get closer to your main purpose, which is personal fulfillment and happiness.

5. Adequate time and energy to attend to personal needs

No one wants to work in a highly-stressful environment that steals away your time from the people and activities that you are dedicating your compensation for. If you know that you are working in order to provide for the comforts of your family or to allow for your recreational hobbies, then you should have a job that gives you ample time to be with the most important people in your life and do the things that you love.

6. Adequate resources and benefits to address your needs

Your job should also provide you with enough compensation that is at least commensurate to your basic needs. Ideally, your compensation should also cover your other financial goals, such as savings and ability to spend for your leisure and a certain degree of luxury.

7. Ability to do the things that you have always wanted

The main reason for your burnout in the workplace is probably not even the management or that annoying colleague you never want to see again. It is most likely just the feeling that you are being forced to do something that you do not want to do. Knowing that you would be more willing to commit to your work, if was your dream job, is a great incentive to go out there and find the type of work you'll actually enjoy and want to work hard at. If you believe that you are a better artist than a desk clerk, then by all means, fulfill your dream of having a career in the arts instead! That way, you can enjoy your work week as much as your weekends, and you'll never think of quitting your job again.

Should You Look for a New Job Immediately?

Quitting your job is a major life decision, and when you feel that you just went through a major life change, it is best to check in with your emotions and your goals first. Think of your old work as a relationship – just because one ended, it does not mean that you should go ahead and look for another one right away.

Give yourself a temporary break without hitting the classified ads quite yet. Give yourself time to recover from burnout, and cater to your personal needs. Take a short vacation, indulge in your hobby, or spend some quality time with your love ones – do anything that will allow you to recover emotionally. That way, you will enable yourself to seek out and find a new job that will logically fit your needs, and not something that would just serve as a temporary solution to your immediate needs, whereby you mind find yourself in a similar situation a few months down the road, wanting to quit.

You should only want to start working immediately if you have a great gig available and you know that it is a job that would cater to most, if not all, of your goals – not only does it have a better paycheck, but it also allows you to have personal time and be involved in the things that you are passionate about. At the same time, make sure that the new job is free from the same problems that you had at your previous workplace. For example, maybe you liked your previous job description just fine, and enjoyed the work you were doing there, so maybe you're actually looking for a similar job, but under better management.

How to Know If You Are Ready to Start Work Again

As a rule, only start looking for employment under a new boss once you feel that you have answered all of the questions earlier in this book, and have a clear direction of what type of work and what type of job you are hunting for that can bring about personal happiness and a sense of fulfillment. Or alternatively, if you are aware that you cannot sustain your finances without working in an office, then you should try to speed up this discovery process and find a job soon, by all means.

You may choose to work for someone else if you do not feel that you are good at managing your own career and you want a work environment that will take care of your career and workflow for you. If you like the business model of another company, and you would be happy and willing to work in that environment, then you may have found the appropriate new workplace.

However, if you are confident that you can build your career on your own, then you may prefer to be your own boss instead, and you should move forward with the process of creating your own company, developing a network of allies, and marketing yourself to your ideal clients. This model is especially attractive if you profile yourself as a resourceful person that can also lead other people given and create a business that would allow you to do the things you are passionate about.

Or, if you believe you can create a job for yourself as a freelancer, and you can offer consultancy instead of being employed full time, then becoming a freelancer or consultant might be a better option for you.

Remember that offices and companies are not the only source of financial freedom, and they are not the only places that can provide you the venue to learn and earn. Choose to be employed if you are aware that you need another person's resources in order to be paid for doing the things that you are good at and you love. Should you be able to find a workplace that enables you to do that, then you have found a suitable job for your needs. When you are certain about exactly what you want and what's best for you, and then you find such a workplace, you are ready to start working again.

Conclusion

Thank you for reading this book!

I hope that this book has served as the perfect guide for you to quit your job and land a better one. More importantly, I hope you now realize that working someplace you don't like, or doing work that you're just not passionate about, is simply unacceptable. You are not a zombie. You are a human that was specifically designed to have certain skills, tastes, and preferences, and you need to be confident in yourself that you can, and will, find a way to earn money doing something that you truly enjoy and are passionate about. Last, I hope that you have found enough knowledge in this book to help identify a new job that you wouldn't want to quit for an extended amount of time – whether that is a freelance career, employment in the best workplace that you can think of, or through creating your own business!

The next step is to make sure that your new job would be flexible enough to meet your changing needs, and to find the passion in work, despite the new stress that is bound to weigh down on you. Once you know what burnout feels like, you'll know you never want to experience it again. The only way to avoid future burnout is to take enough time in figuring out what you really love in order to ensure you'll be working at something you always feel positive about.

Finally, if you have enjoyed this book, I'd really appreciate it if you'd take a moment to rate it at Amazon.com and post a review comment. I look forward to hearing from you!

Made in United States
Orlando, FL
08 December 2024

55189665R00036